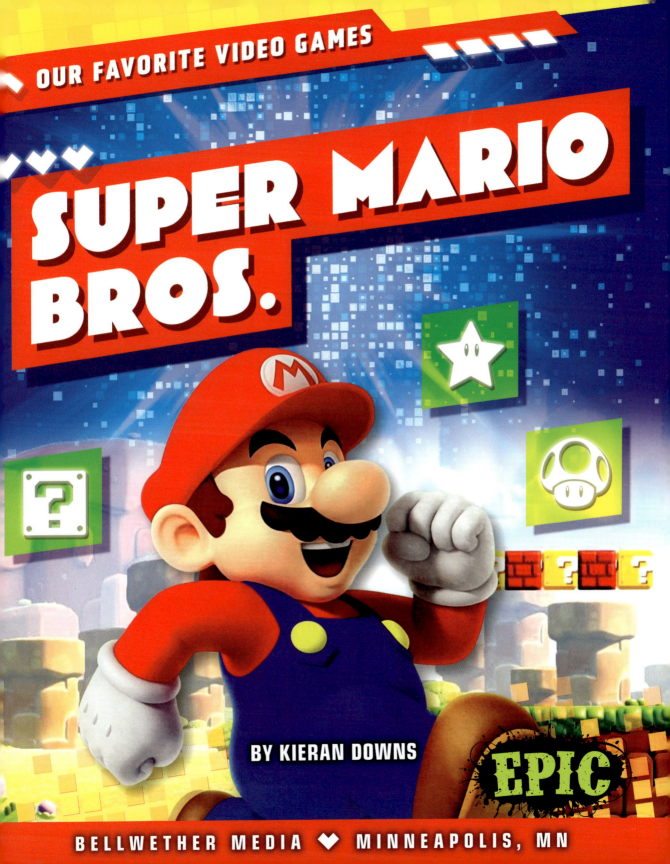

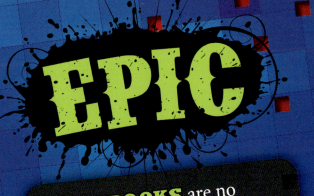

EPIC BOOKS are no ordinary books. They burst with intense action, high-speed heroics, and shadows of the unknown. Are you ready for an Epic adventure?

This is not an official Super Mario Bros. book. It is not approved by or connected with Nintendo.

This edition first published in 2025 by Bellwether Media, Inc.

No part of this publication may be reproduced in whole or in part without written permission of the publisher. For information regarding permission, write to Bellwether Media, Inc., Attention: Permissions Department, 6012 Blue Circle Drive, Minnetonka, MN 55343.

Library of Congress Cataloging-in-Publication Data

Names: Downs, Kieran, author.
Title: Super Mario Bros. / by Kieran Downs.
Description: Minneapolis, MN : Bellwether Media, 2025. | Series: Epic. Our favorite video games | Includes bibliographical references and index. | Audience: Ages 7-12 | Audience: Grades 2-3 | Summary: "Engaging images accompany information about Super Mario Bros. The combination of high-interest subject matter and light text is intended for students in grades 2 through 7"-- Provided by publisher.
Identifiers: LCCN 2024005415 (print) | LCCN 2024005416 (ebook) | ISBN 9798893040500 (library binding) | ISBN 9781644879900 (ebook)
Subjects: LCSH: Super Mario Bros. (Game)--Juvenile literature.
Classification: LCC GV1469.35.S96 D68 2025 (print) | LCC GV1469.35.S96 (ebook) | DDC 794.8--dc23/eng/20240205
LC record available at https://lccn.loc.gov/2024005415
LC ebook record available at https://lccn.loc.gov/2024005416

Text copyright © 2025 by Bellwether Media, Inc. EPIC and associated logos are trademarks and/or registered trademarks of Bellwether Media, Inc. Bellwether Media is a division of Chrysalis Education Group.

Editor: Elizabeth Neuenfeldt   Designer: Gabriel Hilger

Printed in the United States of America, North Mankato, MN.

TABLE OF CONTENTS

FAMILY FUN	4
THE HISTORY OF SUPER MARIO BROS.	8
SUPER MARIO BROS. TODAY	16
SUPER MARIO BROS. FANS	18
GLOSSARY	22
TO LEARN MORE	23
INDEX	24

FAMILY FUN

A family plays *Super Mario Bros. Wonder*. One player hits an item block. An elephant fruit pops out. Mario grabs it. He is now an elephant! He easily breaks through blocks. The family can finish the level!

JUMPMAN

Mario first appeared in 1981. He was in a game called *Donkey Kong*. He was called Jumpman!

SUPER MARIO BROS. WONDER

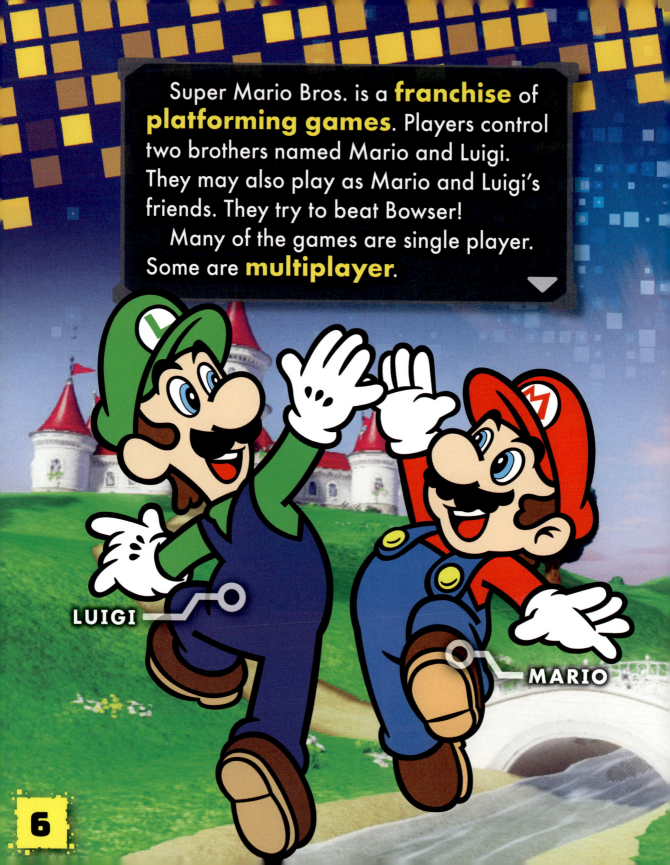

Super Mario Bros. is a **franchise** of **platforming games**. Players control two brothers named Mario and Luigi. They may also play as Mario and Luigi's friends. They try to beat Bowser!

Many of the games are single player. Some are **multiplayer**.

LUIGI

MARIO

❓ IN-GAME POWER UPS

MUSHROOM

FIRE FLOWER

SUPER STAR

ELEPHANT FRUIT

SUPER BELL

TANOOKI SUIT

THE HISTORY OF SUPER MARIO BROS.

SHIGERU MIYAMOTO

Super Mario Bros. was first made by Shigeru Miyamoto. This game was released by Nintendo in 1985.

The game was made for the Nintendo Entertainment System (NES) in the United States. It was a hit!

SUPER MARIO BROS.

DEVELOPER PROFILE

NAME	Nintendo
LOCATION	Kyoto, Japan
YEAR FOUNDED	1889
NUMBER OF EMPLOYEES	7,317 in 2023

By the early 1990s, *Super Mario Bros. 2* and *3* came out. Both **sequels** were popular on the NES.

SUPER MARIO BROS. 2

SUPER MARIO BROS. 3

Soon, *Super Mario World* came out. It was made for the Super Nintendo Entertainment System. It was a hit!

The first **3D** Mario game was *Super Mario 64*. It came out in 1996 on the Nintendo 64.

SUPER MARIO 64

In 2006, *New Super Mario Bros.* came out on the Nintendo DS. It was the first new **2D** Mario game in over 10 years!

SUPER MARIO MAKER

In 2015, *Super Mario Maker* came out on the Wii U. Players could make their own levels.

Super Mario Odyssey came out in 2017. It was a top-selling game on the Nintendo Switch!

SUPER MARIO BROS. TIMELINE

1985
Super Mario Bros. comes out

1990
Super Mario Bros. 3 comes out in the United States

1996
Super Mario 64 comes out

2015
Super Mario Maker comes out

2017
Super Mario Odyssey comes out

15

SUPER MARIO BROS. TODAY

Most Super Mario Bros. games today are played on **consoles**.

SUPER MARIO BROS. GAMES BY SALES

16

Voice of Mario

Charles Martinet was the voice of Mario from 1994 to 2023. In 2023, Kevin Afghani took over the role.

CHARLES MARTINET

BOWSER'S FURY

In 2D Super Mario Bros. games, players run and jump through **side-scrolling** levels. Players look for collectibles in wide-open levels in 3D Super Mario Bros. games.

SUPER MARIO BROS. FANS

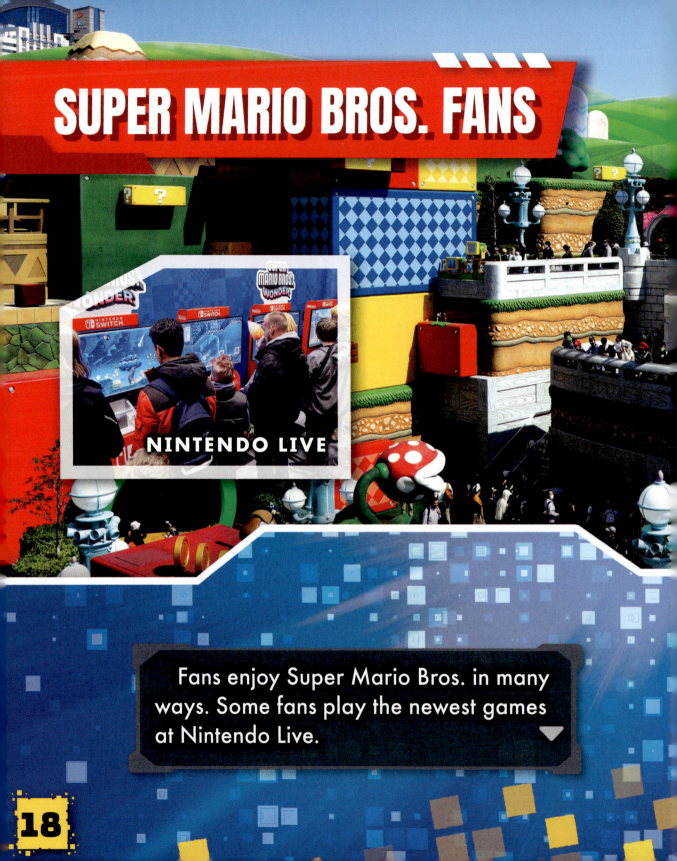

NINTENDO LIVE

Fans enjoy Super Mario Bros. in many ways. Some fans play the newest games at Nintendo Live.

18

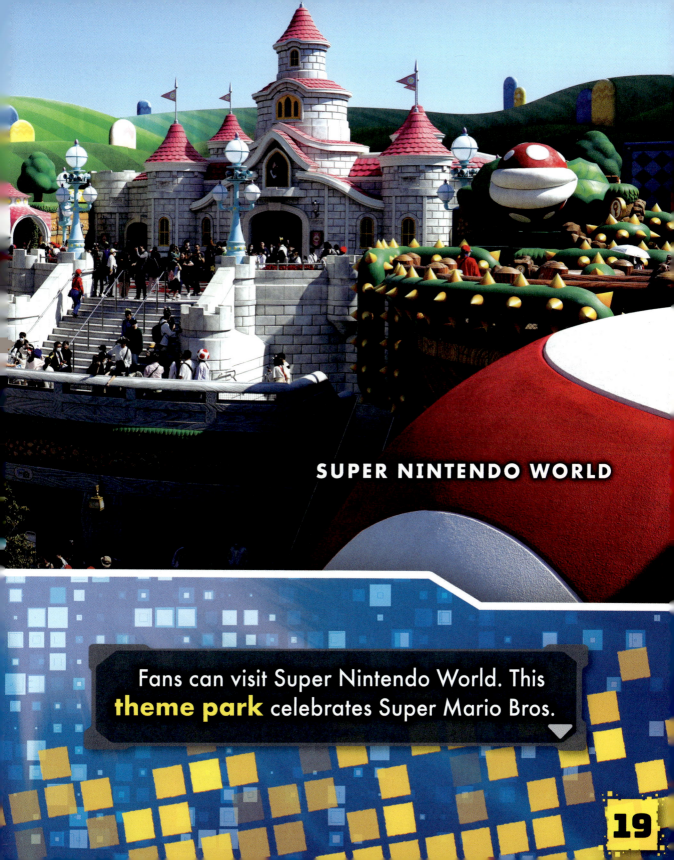

SUPER NINTENDO WORLD

Fans can visit Super Nintendo World. This **theme park** celebrates Super Mario Bros.

In 2023, *The Super Mario Bros. Movie* hit theaters. Fans saw their favorite characters on the big screen. Some fans **speedrun** the games. Fans continue to enjoy Mario and Luigi's adventures!

GAMES DONE QUICK

DATE winter and summer

LOCATION various

EVENT an event where players speedrun games, including Super Mario Bros. games, to raise money for causes

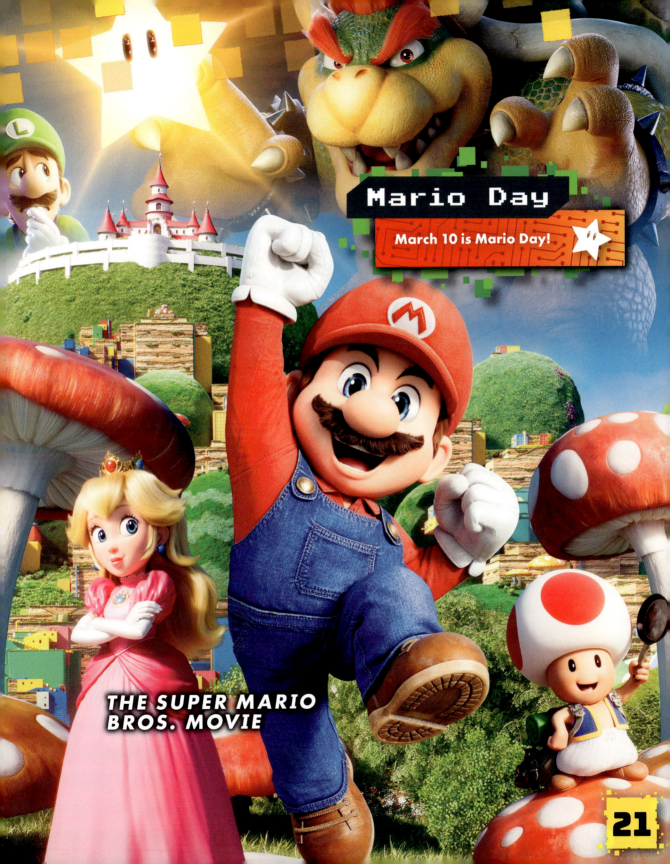

GLOSSARY

2D—related to something that has height and width; players can only move left, right, up, or down in a 2D game.

3D—related to something that has height, width, and depth; players can move in any direction in a 3D game.

consoles—game systems that connect to screens to play video games

franchise—a series of related works that take place in the same world

multiplayer—able to be played by more than one player at a time

platforming games—games where players run and jump their way through levels

sequels—works that continue the story of a previous work

side-scrolling—moving from left to right

speedrun—to finish a video game as quickly as possible

theme park—an amusement park where the rides or activities are based around a certain idea

TO LEARN MORE

AT THE LIBRARY

Neuenfeldt, Elizabeth. *Video Games.* Minneapolis, Minn.: Bellwether Media, 2023.

Rathburn, Betsy. *Video Game Developer.* Minneapolis, Minn.: Bellwether Media, 2023.

Shaw, Gina. *What is Nintendo?* New York, N.Y.: Penguin Workshop, 2021.

ON THE WEB

FACTSURFER

Factsurfer.com gives you a safe, fun way to find more information.

1. Go to www.factsurfer.com.

2. Enter "Super Mario Bros." into the search box and click 🔍.

3. Select your book cover to see a list of related content.

INDEX

2D, 13, 17
3D, 12, 17
Afghani, Kevin, 17
characters, 4, 5, 6, 17, 20
consoles, 9, 10, 11, 12, 13, 14, 16
Donkey Kong, 5
fans, 18, 19, 20
Games Done Quick, 20
history, 5, 8, 9, 10, 11, 12, 13, 14, 15, 20
in-game power ups, 7
Mario Day, 21
Martinet, Charles, 17
Miyamoto, Shigeru, 8
New Super Mario Bros., 13
Nintendo, 8, 9
Nintendo Live, 18

platforming games, 6
players, 4, 6, 14, 17
sales, 16
speedrun, 20
Super Mario 64, 12
Super Mario Bros., 8, 9
Super Mario Bros. 2, 10
Super Mario Bros. 3, 10
Super Mario Bros. Movie, The, 20, 21
Super Mario Bros. Wonder, 4, 5
Super Mario Maker, 14
Super Mario Odyssey, 14
Super Mario World, 11
Super Nintendo World, 19
timeline, 15
United States, 9

The images in this book are reproduced through the courtesy of: Eric Broder Van Dyke, front cover (Mario); Betsy Rathburn, front cover (*Super Mario Bros. Wonder*); Tinxi, p. 3; BSIP SA/ Alamy, p. 4; ilbusca, p. 5 (Jumpman); Gabriel Hilger, pp. 4-5, 7 (mushroom, fire flower, super star, elephant fruit, super bell, tanooki suit), 10 (*Super Mario Bros. 2, Super Mario Bros. 3*), 11 (*Super Mario World*), 12 (*Super Mario 64*), 13 (*New Super Mario Bros.*), 15 (2015, 2017); 16-17; firevectors, p. 6 (Mario and Luigi); UPI/ Alamy, p. 8; pumkinpie/ Alamy, p. 9 (*Super Mario Bros.*); HauLar, p. 9 (Nintendo headquarters); Ian Leonard/ Alamy, p. 13 (Nintendo DS); AP Images for Nintendo of America/ AP Images, pp. 14-15; robtek, p. 15 (1985, 1996); BH-Photo, p. 15 (1990); Brandon Nagy, p. 17 (Charles Martinet); dpa picture alliance/ Alamy, p. 18 (Nintendo Live); Mergeldea, pp. 18-19; Gage Skidmore/ Wikipedia, p. 20; Album/ Alamy, pp. 20-21; Oleg Elkov, p. 23.